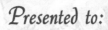

Presented to:

_____

From:

_____

Fresh-Cut Flowers
for a *Friend*

D I A N N A
B O O H E R

WORD PUBLISHING
Dallas·London·Vancouver·Melbourne

Published by Word Publishing,
Dallas, Texas, 75234.

Published in association with the literary agency of Alive Communications,
1465 Kelly Johnson Blvd., Suite 320, Colorado Springs, CO 80920

J. Countryman is a registered trademark of Word Publishing, Inc.

A J. Countryman Book

Designed by Garborg Design Works, Minneapolis, Minnesota

Photos by Lisa Garborg

Edited by Terri Gibbs

ISBN: 0-8499-5274-3

Printed and bound in Belgium.

*You may not be in a class
by yourself, but it sure doesn't
take long to call the roll.*

BUM PHILLIPS

Your friendship is special to me.

Of acquaintances, there are many.

Of casual friends, there are many.

But close friends—they are few.

*A friend is
someone
you can do
nothing with,
and enjoy it.*

ANONYMOUS

When I think about the times
we've spent together, the best
memories are those when
we did nothing special.
We simply talked, walked, lived.

We can do not great things; only small things with great love.

MOTHER TERESA

In thinking about our friendship, it's not the big things that stand out. It's the many, many small things that show how much you care.

Friendship is unnecessary,
like philosophy, like art....
It has no survival value;
rather it is one of those things
that give value to survival.

C. S. LEWIS

I could live without friends.
But what a depressing
thought! A friendship like
ours gives definition to that
old phrase "the good life."

*Do not forsake
your own friend or
your father's friend,
nor go to your
brother's house in
the day of your
calamity; better
is a neighbor
nearby than a
brother far away.*

PROVERBS 27:10

I have counted on you like family.
Thanks for taking their place
in so many times of need.

*True friendship is a
plant of slow growth.*

GEORGE WASHINGTON

A conversation here.
A conversation there. A meal.
A trip. A visit. A problem faced.
A struggle overcome. A success
shared. Little by little, our
friendship has grown.

The world is so empty if
one thinks only of mountains,
rivers, and cities; but to know
someone here and there who
thinks and feels with us, and
who, though distant, is close
to us in spirit, this makes the
earth an inhabited garden.

GÓETHE

Friends don't have to say hello or good-bye. Like a neighbor who pops in to borrow a cup of sugar, you can pop back into my life in a day or a year and it's as though we've never missed a beat.

Love is blind;
friendship closes
its eyes.

ANONYMOUS

Some people take their
friends as a "project," trying to
mold them and remake them.
Thank you for accepting me
for who I am.

Lots of people want to ride with you in the limo, but what you want is someone who will take the bus with you when the limo breaks down.

OPRAH WINFREY

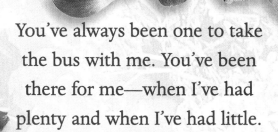

You've always been one to take the bus with me. You've been there for me—when I've had plenty and when I've had little.

13

*Friendship is a horizon—
which expands whenever
we approach it.*

E. R. HAZLIP

Thank you for stretching me.
For helping me to see
new ways of relating,
new causes to consider,
new interests to explore.

*Friendship multiplies
the good of life and
divides the evil.*

BALTASAR GRACIAN

Sharing the happy-nings
in my life with you
has doubled my pleasure.
The same is true for the
disappointments—you've
made the doldrums
more bearable.

*Friends are relatives
you make for yourself.*

EUSTACHE DESCHAMPS

We don't choose our
families, but friends
are up for grabs.
I'm glad to choose you.
You are as close as
family—if not closer.

*Silences make the real
conversations between friends.
Not the saying but the never
needing to say is what counts.*

MARGARET RUNBECK

Silences are never awkward
with you. We share quiet
companionship without
having to make excuses.
I'm comfortable with that.

You don't just luck into things as much as you'd like to think you do. You build step by step, whether it's friendships or opportunities.

BARBARA BUSH

I don't think it was luck
that our paths crossed.
Your friendship is one
of God's gifts designed
especially for me.

Only your real
friends will tell you when
your face is dirty.

SICILIAN PROVERB

Thank you for saying things
to me that have not always
been easy to say. You risk my
hurt, disappointment, and
anger. But you say them
anyway. I appreciate that.

There is a friend who sticks closer than a brother.

PROVERBS 18:24

The most important thing
we share is our faith. When
either of us feels totally alone,
let's pledge to remind each
other of God's love.

The bird a nest,
the spider a web,
man friendship.

WILLIAM BLAKE

You are my hearth
on cold winter days.

Better to be a nettle
in the side of your
friend than his echo.

RALPH WALDO
EMERSON

At times, I've taken great
liberty in telling you what
I think. Maybe I've said
what you didn't really want
to hear. But thank you for
listening anyway.

*We should get into
the habit of reading
inspirational books,
looking at inspirational
pictures, hearing
inspirational music,
associating with
inspirational friends.*

ALFRED A.
MONTAPERT

Like great music, art, literature,
and nature . . . you inspire me.

There can be
no friendship
without confi-
dence, and
no confidence
without integrity.

SAMUEL
JOHNSON

Thank you for being loyal to me,
for holding my secrets safe.
I trust you implicitly.

When a friend is in trouble, don't annoy him by asking if there is anything you can do. Think up something appropriate and do it.

EDGAR WATSON HOWE

Without my ever having
to ask, you always seem
to know just what to do.
That makes it doubly nice—
what you've done and what
I didn't have to ask.

As iron sharpens iron,

so a man sharpens the

countenance of his friend.

PROVERBS 27:17

You read between
the lines when I'm not
being transparent.
You push me beyond the
borders of mediocrity.

*I value the friend
who for me finds time
on his calendar,
but I cherish the friend
who for me does not
consult the calendar.*

ROBERT BRAULT

Thanks for always
making my calls
and visits welcome.

*Wishing to
be friends is
quick work, but
friendship is
slow-ripening
fruit.*

ARISTOTLE

I like the little rituals
and inside jokes we share.
They weave our past
together tightly and
promise joys for tomorrow.

When we are young,
friends are, like everything else,
a matter of course.
In the old days we know
what it means to have them.

EDWARD GRIEG

When I was growing up a friend was someone to talk with at recess and do things with on the weekends. But as I've gotten older, my friends have come to mean so much more. They are not pastimes— they are the main events.

*The proper office of a friend
is to side with you when
you are in the wrong.
Nearly anybody will side with
you when you are right.*

MARK TWAIN

Thanks for speaking up for
me and for taking my side—
even when it is not the
popular thing to do. Loyalty
rates high in my book.

*Faithful are the wounds
of a friend, but the kisses
of an enemy are deceitful.*

PROVERBS 27:6

You are not always
easy on me. And that's
exactly what I need.
Sometimes I feel
that you are the voice
of God in my life.

A friend is a person with whom I may be sincere. Before him I may think aloud.

RALPH WALDO EMERSON

I'm glad I don't have to censor my thoughts with you. Certainly everything that runs through my mind shouldn't come out my mouth—but with you, I'm safe. You're a great sounding board.

*In every friend we
lose a part of ourselves,
and the best part.*

ALEXANDER POPE

I hope that through our
friendship I've enriched your
life in some small way.
You have certainly made me
richer by far. You've soaked
up my heart and "translated"
me to the world.

*A friend is one who
takes me for what I am.*

HENRY DAVID THOREAU

We've gone through
emotional highs and
emotional lows.
Our friendship is not
threatened by either—
it grows with both.

*A merry heart does good,
like a medicine.*

PROVERBS 17:22

You make me laugh—
even when life
is far from funny.

Men kick friendship
around like a football,
but it doesn't seem to crack.
Women treat it like glass
and it goes to pieces.

ANNE MORROW
LINDBERGH

I'm glad that our
friendship is not fragile.

STAY is a charming word in a friend's vocabulary.

AMOS BRONSON
ALCOTT

Too many times, with some
of my ongoing conflicts
and issues, you've stayed until
the wee hours to hear me out,
and it's in those times that
you've meant the most.

*We challenge
each other
to be funnier
and smarter.*

ANNIE
GOTTLIEB

Thanks for all the great
laughter we've shared.
You have a wonderful
sense of always seeing
the lighter side of life.

Depth of friendship
does not depend upon
length of acquaintance.

RABINDRANATH
TAGORE

True friendship
is not measured
in days or decades.

Two are better than one,
because they have a good
reward for their labor. For if
they fall, one will lift up his
companion. But woe to him
who is alone when he falls, for
he has no one to help him up.

ECCLESIASTES 4:9-10

In so many situations, you have
been the difference between
failure and success for me.
Thank you for being my backup.
We make a great team!

*A friend is a present
you give yourself.*

ROBERT LOUIS
STEVENSON

Every time we get together,
it feels like Christmas morning!

*A mirror reflects
a man's face,
but what he
is really like is
shown by the
kind of friends
he chooses.*

PROVERBS
27:19 TLB

I'm proud to have you
call me "friend"—it's a badge
I wear with honor.

*If there is any sin
more deadly than envy, it is
being pleased at being envied.*

RICHARD ARMOUR

There doesn't seem to be an
envious bone in your body!
Thanks for being successful and
happy enough in your own right
that you can enjoy the good
things that come my way.

46

He who covers a transgression seeks love, but he who repeats a matter separates friends.

PROVERBS 17:9

You don't simmer with sympathy over my weaknesses; you summon my strengths. I'm a better person because of you.

*A mere friend will agree
with you, but a real friend
will argue.*

RUSSIAN PROVERB

With some friends, I talk work.
With some, I talk family.
With some, I talk pastimes.
But with you, there's no subject
too big or too small.

*A friend is one who takes
you to lunch even though
you are not tax deductible.*

UNKNOWN

As schedules get tighter and days
seem to get shorter, there's a
temptation to sacrifice friendship
for family or business. How sad!
. . . How about lunch?

*The pleasantness
of one's friend springs from
his earnest counsel.*

PROVERBS 27:9

How wonderful to have a
wise friend like you. When I can't
see the forest for the trees,
you pull back the leaves and say,
"Look again."

A faithful friend is an image of God.

FRENCH PROVERB

Someone has said that God has
no hands but ours . . . no feet but
ours. Sometimes you are God's
hands and feet in my life.

Friendship lies on a long continuum of intensity.

THOMAS MOORE

Our friendship ebbs
and flows in its intensity.
When I have a problem
that pulls me ashore like
the tide, you move toward
me like a swift current
to offer concern.
When I'm feeling free
and independent, you let me
ride the waves alone.

Friendship based solely upon gratitude is like a photograph; with time it fades.

CARMEN SYLVA

Our friendship rests
on the best, not the worst,
in both of us. We both
bring to the table wisdom—
only on different topics.

*A gossip separates
close friends.*

PROVERBS 16:28

When I listen to the news,
watch television, or read
the paper, it seems the
whole world runs on gossip.
Thank you for always
believing the best about me
and not letting someone's
idle words ruin my reputation
or our relationship.

We are all travelers in the wilderness of this world, and the best that we find in our travels is an honest friend.

ROBERT LOUIS
STEVENSON

You understand the
contradictions in me that
sometimes cause others to
misunderstand me. With you,
I can breathe more freely.

A true friend is somebody who can make us do what we can.

RALPH WALDO
EMERSON

I'm often tempted to give up on
myself or my dream too soon.
Thank you for encouraging me
to reach for the stars.

*I have
learned that
to be with
those I like
is enough.*

WALT
WHITMAN

Leisure time is too precious these days to waste with those whose company we don't enjoy. In case I haven't said so pointedly, I enjoy spending time with you.

Never injure a friend,
even in jest.

CICERO

You have never hurt me by
what you've said or done.
And that's a claim few can
make—even family.

*Before you can help
make the world right,
you must be
made right within.*

JOHN MILLER

Our friendship has not
been by chance. God sent
you into my life for
a special purpose. Thanks for
being His friend to me.

*The refining pot is for silver
and the furnace for gold,
and a man is valued by what
others say of him.*

PROVERBS 27:21

I appreciate all the uplifting
things you say about me
and my efforts. But as
my friend, please don't ever
let me become full of myself.

*The better part of one's life
consists of his friendships.*

ABRAHAM LINCOLN

When I consider my past—all my
memories as a child, as a youth,
and as an adult—the most vivid
memories are not of events but
of friends. I've come to mark and
measure my life by the friends
I've been privileged to know.

Friendship is the inexpressible comfort of feeling safe with a person, having neither to weigh thoughts nor measure words.

GEORGE ELLIOT

I treasure our talks.
That emotional connection is
vital to my well-being.

It is one of the blessings of old friends that you can afford to be stupid with them.

RALPH WALDO
EMERSON

I've done and said some crazy things in your presence. It feels so comfortable not to have to worry about how I'm coming across with you. I can try out new ideas for your honest reaction.

*The real secret
of happiness is
not what you
give or what you
receive; it's what
you share.*

UNKNOWN

I am so grateful that you share
your life with me—the small
events, the casual thoughts, the
deepest heartaches.

A heart at peace gives
life to the body,
but envy rots the bones.

PROVERBS
14:30 NIV

When I tell you of the happiness
in my life, one look at your face
tells me there's not an ounce
of envy in you. Thanks for
being such a true friend.

Friendship demands attention.

THOMAS MOORE

You show courtesy ... you do
not impose ... you ask first ...
you listen quietly ... you stay
late ... you arrive early ...
you help without being
asked ... you make time.

Some of the most rewarding and beautiful moments of a friendship happen in the unforeseen open spaces between planned activities. It is important that you allow these spaces to exist.

CHRISTINE
LEEFELDT

How long has it been since
we've spent an entire day
together? Much too long.
You have a way of renewing my
energy and enthusiasm for life.

*It takes great generosity
to accept generosity.*

MERLE SHAIN

Thank you for letting me
give to you in small ways
and in big ways.
All of us grow by giving.

*All that is not eternal
is out of date.*

C.S. LEWIS

I admire your attention to
the important rather than
the trivial. Your life is
constantly lived to lay up
treasures in heaven.

*Friendship is one of the sweetest
joys of life. Many might have
failed beneath the bitterness of their
trial had they not found a friend.*

CHARLES SPURGEON

Friendship satisfies a longing
that no other relationship
can match. I feel disconnected
when I am separated from
close friends like you.

True friendship is like sound health, the value of it is seldom known until it is lost.

C.C. COLTON

I don't want to take you for granted. Please know how much I appreciate our friendship. I'll cherish our easy relationship always.

Friends are like windows through which you see out into the world and back into yourself....If you don't have friends you see much less than you otherwise might.

MERLE SHAIN

Thanks for being my eyes and ears on the world. I benefit from your interactions with others. Your network eventually becomes my network; your perspective, my perspective.

*Friendship is
like money,
easier made
than kept.*

SAMUEL BUTLER

Can you believe we've been
friends for so long? As with
any other great achievement,
I feel like celebrating!

*A friend loves
at all times, and
a brother is born
for adversity.*

PROVERBS 17:17

Maybe the
one good thing
in a difficult day
is finding out
how much we need
our friends.

Friendship

is a

sheltering

tree.

SAMUEL
TAYLOR
COLERIDGE

Our friendship provides me
with plenty of choices.
You never make me feel guilty
when I have to say no.

He who throws away a
friend is as bad as he
who throws away his life.

SOPHOCLES

Someone has said that sooner
or later we outgrow our friends.
I disagree. Though the stages
of friendships change, our
friendship will last a lifetime.

There is no friend like an old friend
Who has shared our morning days,
No greeting like his welcome,
No homage like his praise.

OLIVER WENDELL HOLMES

Thank you for always taking the
time to offer compliments.
Words of praise coming from
you mean a lot because I value
your opinion so deeply.

A blessed thing it is for any man or woman to have a friend, one human soul whom we can trust utterly, who knows the best and worst of us, and who loves us in spite of all our faults.

CHARLES KINGSLEY

You have certainly
seen and heard
the worst in me—
and yet, you still
call me your friend.

*To hear complaints with
patience, even when
complaints are vain, is one
of the duties of friendship.*

SAMUEL JOHNSON

Don't you wish you had
a dollar for each minute you've
listened to me grumble about
this or that? Rest assured that
your listening has not been
wasted. My telling you kept me
from telling the rest of the world!

*One of the most beautiful
qualities of true friendship is to
understand and to be understood.*

SENECA

Raising our children. Dealing
with our parents. Relating to our
spouses. Detail upon detail.
Conversation after conversation.
Event after event. With one
experience piling upon another,
I've concluded that for each
other we are one of life's
necessities.

*Friendship...is the golden
thread that ties the hearts
of all hearts of all the world.*

JOHN EVELYN

Thank you for all the time you
have spent pondering my
concerns, pacing the floor,
waiting for the phone to ring
to hear my latest news. Time
is a wonderful gift you have
given me over and over again.

If, instead of a gem or even a flower,
we would cast the gift of a lovely
thought into the heart of a friend,
that would be giving as angels give.

GEORGE
MACDONALD

Our friendship is more
than spending time together.
Our hearts match. You have
touched my life deeply.

The best mirror is an old friend.

GEORGE HERBERT

Thank you for respecting my opinion enough to ask for it often. You and I are down-to-earth, practical, helpful to each other—the things from which long-standing friendships grow.

We cannot tell the precise moment
when friendship is formed.
As in filling a vessel drop by drop,
there is at last a drop which makes
it run over; so in a series of
kindnesses there is at last one
which makes the heart run over.

SAMUEL JOHNSON

When did we become such
good friends? It's difficult
to pinpoint the day or situation.
All I know is that one morning
I awoke and noticed how
important you had become
to my life.

Friendship is like two
clocks keeping time.

UNKNOWN

When we first met,
I knew we would be
perfect friends.
We're exactly
the opposite in
so many ways.
We complement
each other because of it.

The best friend is the man who in wishing me well wishes it for my sake.

ARISTOTLE

Thanks for being the
resident optimist in my life.

*Our friendship brings
sunshine to the shade,
and shade to the sunshine.*

THOMAS BURKE

You never call attention to all
the little things you do for
me—but I notice just the same.

*Our friends show us
what we can do;
our enemies teach us
what we must do.*

GÓETHE

Competitors compare,
contrast, coax, and coerce.
As my friend, you do not take
pride in my defeat; you
applaud my successes.

*A friend is one who
walks in when the rest
of the world walks out.*

WALTER WINCHELL

At times, I've felt totally and
utterly alone. Even when
I didn't openly acknowledge
your friendship, thank you
for waiting in the background
until I reached out.

*A friend is one to whom one can
pour out all the contents of one's heart,
chaff and grain together, knowing that
the gentlest of hands will take and sift it,
keep what is worth keeping, and, with the
breath of kindness, blow the rest away.*

ARABIAN PROVERB

In all the time we've known
each other, you've never
taken unfair advantage of our
relationship. Thank you
for always wanting what
is best for me.

*The only way to have
a friend is to be one.*

RALPH WALDO EMERSON

Thank you for all the lovely
compliments you've given me
during our friendship. You make
me feel good about myself.